Book

MW01484092

Has it ever happened with you, that before you enter a big interview or presentation you had been preparing for, for months now, you hear a voice telling you to just call it quits? You look for the source of it and it turns out, it is coming from within you? People, it is time to meet your inner critic. It tells you to run to some far off land, dump your phone in the water and be free from the shackles of worldly chaos and worries!

We have all been there, and trust us, it is hard to silence that inner critic, step inside the office or conference hall, and give it our best shot. Being an adult and knowing how to deal with such emotions and feeling like giving up is torturous; just imagine what goes on into the little minds of our children when they are faced with a similar task?

In *How Parents Can Teach Children to Counter Negative Thoughts*, we explore the impact of negativity, anxiety, and stress on children and how, as their parents, we can help them cope and have a positive outlook towards life.

We look at the various dynamics and factors that breed negative thinking and use tools like strong will power, emotional intelligence, and self-esteem boosting strategies to help them develop habits that will ensure they are prepared for the world. With science-backed practices and tips, written in a simple and comprehensible manner, this is a brief guide for parents who need assistance dealing with children who have a negative attitude.

How Parents Can Teach Children to Counter Negative Thoughts

Channelling Your Child's Negativity, Self-Doubt, and Anxiety into Resilience, Willpower, and Determination

Frank Dixon

professional advice. The content within this book has been derived from various sources. Please consult a licensed professional before attempting any techniques outlined in this book.

By reading this document, the reader agrees that under no circumstances is the author responsible for any losses, direct or indirect, that are incurred as a result of the use of the information contained within this document, including, but not limited to, errors, omissions, or inaccuracies.

OTHER BOOKS BY FRANK DIXON

How Parents Can Raise Resilient Children: Preparing Your Child for the Real Tough World of Adulthood by Instilling Them With Principles of Love, Self-Discipline, and Independent Thinking

❀ ❀ ❀

How Parents Can Teach Children To Counter Negative Thoughts: Channelling Your Child's Negativity, Self-Doubt and Anxiety Into Resilience, Willpower and Determination

❀ ❀ ❀

The Vital Parenting Skills and Happy Children Box Set: A 5 Full-Length Parenting Book Compilation for Raising Happy Kids Who Are Honest, Respectful and Well-Adjusted

❀ ❀ ❀

The 7 Vital Parenting Skills and Confident Kids Box Set: A 7 Full-Length Positive Parenting Book Compilation for Raising Well-Adjusted Children

❀ ❀ ❀

**For a complete list, please visit
http://bestparentingbooks.org/books**

YOUR FREE GIFT

Before we begin, I have something special waiting for you. Another action-paced book, free of cost. Think of it as my way of saying thank you to you for purchasing this.

Your gift is a special PDF actionable guide titled, ***"Profoundly Positive Parenting: Learn the Top 10 Skills to Raising Extraordinary Kids!"***

As the title suggests, it's a collection of 10 parenting skills that will help you pave the way towards raising amazing and successful children. It's short enough to read quickly, but meaty enough to offer actionable advice that can make impactful changes to the way you parent.

Intrigued, I knew you would be!

Claim your copy of Profoundly Positive Parenting by clicking on the link below and join my mailing list:

http://bestparentingbooks.org/free-gift/

PROFOUNDLY

POSITIVE PARENTING

Learn the Top 10 Parenting Skills
to Raising Extraordinary Kids!

FRANK DIXON

Before we jump in, I'd like to express my gratitude. I know this mustn't be the first book you came across and yet you still decided to give it a read. There are numerous courses and guides you could have picked instead that promise to make you an ideal and well-rounded parent while raising your children to be the best they can be.

But for some reason, mine stood out from the rest and this makes me the happiest person on the planet right now. If you stick with it, I promise this will be a worthwhile read.

In the pages that follow, you're going to learn the best parenting skills so that your child can grow to become the best version of themselves and in doing so experience a meaningful understanding of what it means to be an effective parent.

Notable Quotes About Parenting

"Children Must Be Taught How To Think,
Not What To Think."

— **Margaret Mead**

"It's easier to build strong children than to fix
broken men [or women]."

- Frederick Douglass

"Truly great friends are hard to find, difficult
to leave, and impossible to forget."

— **George Randolf**

"Nothing in life is to be feared, it is only to be
understood. Now is the time to understand
more, so that we may fear less."

— **Scientist Marie Curie**

Table of Contents

Introduction

Hey, you!

Are you up for some story time? Well, here's one you are going to remember for a long, long time!

It was the 1980s. In a school in Tennessee, one of the teachers, while teaching a class complained of something smelling "gasoline-like." As soon as she made that claim, she started to get sick. She felt short of breath, had nausea, a headache and also reported dizziness. Almost everyone in her class started to exhibit the same symptoms and before you know it, the whole school was stricken.

Firefighters were called upon to the scene and the school was evacuated. The police and ambulances also arrived and by evening, some 80 students and 19 teachers and staff members were admitted to the local emergency room, of which, 38 stayed overnight at the hospital.

After several inspections at the school and investigations by Government agencies, the authorities were unable to find any traces of gas leaks. The blood reports of the admitted patients didn't show any toxic substances or gases in their system. As it turns out, the fear of "being poisoned" had fueled the symptoms in the kids and staff members.

1

According to one of the epidemiologists, the outbreak was due to a phenomenon we now come to know as mass psychogenic illness. This happens when the fear of infection is as deadly as the disease itself and tricks the brain into thinking that the disease has been acquired and thus, it starts to show symptoms commonly associated with it. The students too had perceived that there was some threat plaguing them and thus started to show similar symptoms.

This tells us two things. First, our mind is a remarkable and stupid thing. On one end, it allows us to explore so much in the universe, store and process so much information at once and yet, sometimes, so stupid to get tricked in this way. Second, it shows us the power of fear and negative thinking and what it can do to the human brain.

Fear–as old as humans themselves–is a deeply wired reaction that allows us to protect ourselves against threats and dangers. It is what kept the cavemen alive for many years without forming tribes, and it still grips us by the throat when something unexpected comes our way. And believe it or not, we revere it. If we didn't, we wouldn't have dedicated a whole day of celebration to it.

It is fear that breeds negative thoughts–not just in adults but also in kids. Negative thoughts are the worst enemy of a bright and creative mind. Most kids are intrinsically artistic and creative. They have congenital confidence that they are the rulers of the world. Everyone around them is always wanting them to have the best, look the best, and eat the best. Don't we, as parents, have the same? We want them to have the best of both worlds, fulfill their lifelong dreams, live up to set expectations, and follow their dreams without an ounce of self-doubt and fear in the minds.

But what can we do to ensure that they get all of the things mentioned without losing their confidence or giving in to negative thoughts? In this book, we are going to help parents guide and prepare their children for a better and confident tomorrow. We want parents to be able to teach their children resilience, the power of self-discipline, and determination. We want parents to nurture confidence, strong-mindedness, and emotional intelligence in them so that they can counter and whitewash negative thinking from the core.

Chapter 1: Into the Child's Mind

A child's brain is an amazing thing. It is like a whole universe, just waiting to be explored and discovered. Did you know, until the last decade, scientists and researchers believed that children were just miniature versions of adults? They, for the longest time, believed that their minds functioned in the same manner as that of an adult and it is only a matter of time that they learned new skills and practiced their skills. But since this belief doesn't hold true, we see children depicting behaviors we wouldn't observe in an adult. Things like crying over something insignificant or holding onto grudges. Although adults might do something similar, they have a way of convincing themselves of the other positive things out there. Kids, not so much. If they are fixated on something, well that's it then.

Granted, there is nothing wrong with having a strong and determined mind from an early age. However, it can become a problem if that mind is determined to host negative thoughts. Negative thoughts like body-image issues, lack of confidence, low self-esteem, etc., are things that breed negativity on a larger scale. When not discouraged from having such thoughts or paying heed to them, it can land kids in unthinkable troubles in academia, social, and their future professional lives. When they keep submitting to negativity, they rarely focus on the good and thus, lead a life full of disappointments, heartbreaks, and mental health issues.

Even in our wildest dreams, we wouldn't want to raise kids as such. So in this first chapter, we are going to be looking at what negative thoughts are, their types, and then explore why some kids find it so easy to just give up.

What Are Negative Thoughts?

Negative thinking is a whirlpool of thoughts that leads to people finding the worst in everything. It also means these people might reduce their expectations so low that their minds only come up with the worst-case scenarios. It is like a web, each thought connected with newer thoughts developing every second. Imagine this: your child has been asked to play a small role in a school play. It is a small part with almost zero dialogue. All your child has to do is stand on one side, wearing the costume of a tree. Your child is naturally shy and thinks that they will not be able to pull it off.

"Can you tell Ms. Nora that I won't be able to perform in the play?"

"But why?"

"I don't think I can do it. What if I make a fool out of myself? What if I vomit or faint on the stage? Everyone will laugh at me. They will call me a loser

forever. I will have no friends and no one will ever forget it."

Notice how the child is thinking the worst and how each thought is just a continuation of the previous one like a vicious thread? This is what negative thinking looks like. It shatters a child's confidence and makes them believe that they are good for nothing. It can manifest in a pattern of worry, stress, and depression over time.

Many kids are prone to negative thinking. It is what leads them to have meltdowns, engage in fights, and make risky decisions. When they are young, they aren't able to comprehend the many thoughts in their head but as they grow older and reach early adolescence, they begin to associate connections. For instance, they learn that a normal behavior to exhibit when sad is crying. They learn that sometimes when they are anxious or stressed, they turn to bite their nails or pace back and forth in a room. These are all natural reactions to stressful or disturbing situations. However, a reaction is different from behavior. While the former is more natural, the latter isn't. It is more of a choice. How we choose to behave, address, and process what is going on is what we refer to as our 'behavior.'

To teach any behavior, it has to be repeated enough times that it turns into a habit–something you do unintentionally, like putting your hand on your mouth when yawning, or closing your eyes when faced with danger or horror.

Therefore, as parents, we need to instill such habits in our kids that will automatically help them to navigate their way to positivity and optimism.

Negative thinking works on two principles:

1. It disqualifies the positive. Meaning, it dismisses any positive thought or acknowledgment in our head and takes us back to thinking illogically. We only see the negatives with clarity.
2. It maximizes the negative and minimizes the positive. So instead of looking at our positive achievements, we magnify our losses and failures, even if they are small.

There are many different ways of how negativity can manifest itself. It mostly comes in one or more of the following forms.

- Cynicism: This is the most common and usually denotes that your child has a general distrust for people. They have a difficult time listening to people who are trying to encourage them and doubt their motives instead.
- Hostility: Hostility is usually prominent in adolescents and teenagers. As their bodies grow, the chemical imbalances and hormonal changes often lead to mood swings. They develop feelings of unfriendliness towards others and become hesitant in opening up or developing new relationships.

- Polarized Thinking: This way of thinking usually suggests that if a child thinks they are not good at something, say playing the piano or math, then they think they are horrible. They don't believe in being average and don't make any effort to become better at it. It's black or white for them.

- Filtering: This is rather self-explanatory. Kids only notice the bad—or worse—they magnify it in their minds.

- Jump to Conclusions: Some children are quick to assume the worst in things. If something remotely scary comes their way, they take no time in thinking about the worst-case scenarios. They think nothing good can come out of a bad situation ever.

- Blaming: Kids with negativity corrupting their minds also find it easier to blame others for their own maladies. They often take the role of the victim in everything, thinking nothing fair ever happens to them.

- Heaven's Reward Fallacy: They are staunch believers that if they work hard or sacrifice, they will be rewarded. However, when that reward doesn't come, they take to depression and bitterness. An example of this looks something like this: your child studies hard for exams and pulls all-nighters. However, when the result is out, they don't score well. So the next time, they don't work hard at all.

Why It's Easy to Just Give Up

Giving up is sometimes the easiest thing to do. As adults, we are ourselves guilty of this habit, so we don't get to simply tell our kids not to. Many people, children included, give up because they can't face the stress and pain associated with something and they'd rather put an end to the misery. We choose not to endanger our comfort and step out to make sacrifices, all for some uncertain future. Doesn't seem like a very wise bargain, does it?

But do you know why we must always bet against the odds? It is because there is one thing more damaging and hurtful and that is regret. If you don't try, regret will always follow. If you don't encourage your kids to try and never quit, then they will always regret it later. It is an unwanted feeling that keeps us stuck in the past. Had I chosen to take that course during my semester break, I would have been promoted. Had I learned a unique skill, it would have helped me get the job. Had I chosen to follow my passion for sports, I could have made a blooming career out of it.

We don't want our children to live with regrets. Let's say, they are giving up something because the goal doesn't seem appealing. Let's say it is revising everything that has been taught at school. They say that it is too tiring and time-consuming and they would rather spend their time playing outdoors or on a game on their tablet. They promise you that they will start studying once the finals are near and make it up.

9

For the following days, they will feel relieved that they don't have to do it anymore. Might even enjoy the free time for a few weeks, but then what? They will have regrets a few months later when they have to study for the finals and spend hours in their room, sunken in their books. Not to mention, the additional stress and pressure of learning about so much in such a short period. That is when the regret will settle in and make them panic. That is when they will start to hate themselves and a little bit of you too, for not pushing them hard enough to stick with the studying. Not only that, but they also will not be able to perform their best and pass the class with decent grades.

There are several reasons why kids find giving up easy. Let's discuss a few.

They don't have a strong 'Why?'

Did you know, Walt Disney was fired several times and told that he had no original ideas and lacked imagination? Had he chosen to give up, we wouldn't have the world of Disney and the amazing shows we grew up watching.

Like Mr. Walt, some kids don't have a compelling reason to keep going. They lack the answer to that 'why' that our brain keeps asking us as we work towards a goal. When the answer isn't powerful enough, we are likely to give up.

Expecting Fast Results

Some kids, although not suffering from ADHD, just want things to move at a fast pace. They want quick results and are rarely willing to do the work when it comes to something detail-oriented. They are also the ones who resort to taking shortcuts. Shortcuts work, no doubt about that, but not always. And when things don't go as planned, meltdowns and frustration are bound to happen.

As parents, we have to make them patient and have a more stable and calm mindset. We must let them know that not all goals can be achieved in a short period and thus, they must continue to work for them without getting disheartened. Some may have gotten it easy and have things presented to them on a silver plate, but life isn't fair to all and that is okay. A classic example of this can be your teenager trying to lose weight to look a certain way but wanting quick results. So, they resort to quick fixes and aren't willing to do the actual work. They starve themselves, boycott all carbs and later, complain of dizziness and poor concentration and energy levels.

Presuming They Have Unique Problems

A lot of kids presume that no one will understand what they are going through because their problems are so unique. Oh, really? Are you the first-ever child to be bullied at school? Are you the first-ever human to have been compared to an older sibling or cousin?

Are you the first-ever individual to have broken up with a friend or a partner?

Kids who assume they have unique problems fail to see the larger picture. They think that what they are going through is something their parents, peers, or friends won't understand. So, they bother not to speak about them or find solutions.

Doubting Capabilities

Some kids just don't find that push within themselves to bring ideas to fruition. It isn't that they aren't smart, they just lack confidence and believe that they will be ridiculed or made fun of. A lack of confidence in our abilities often halts us from trying new things. Many kids, doubting their skills and abilities abandon their long-term goals. Here's the thing: if you don't have the right mindset and you are always listening to your inner critic, you will be pushing away a lot of valuable things in life. Therefore, we parents have to ensure that our kids don't feel discouraged and fail to fulfill their dreams and aspirations. We have to be their encouragement and that push that makes them want to see what's at the bottom of the cliff and later, dive their way through the crest and trough of life. We have to remind them how wholesome it can feel to achieve their goals and make them experience the joy that comes with it.

One Failure Wears Them Down

Why are kids so quick to give up, you ask? They think that if they are putting their heart and soul into something, it should come out right. Be it a school project, an assignment, or an exam. However, one failure is enough to get them off track and concoct negative thoughts. Failure too can be rewarding. You learn from your mistakes and rethink strategies from a different angle. It piques curiosity and can also serve as a motivation to try harder. Besides, achieving something isn't always on the cards. For some kids, it comes a little late and for some it never does. In both these cases, as parents, we have to make them see the bright side of things and prevent them from going into self-doubt.

Kids who are quick to give in whenever they come across the first stumbling block can take more time in training and developing positive habits. But, it isn't impossible.

Lack of Self-Discipline and Resilience in Life

Some kids give up easily because they lack the discipline required to stay patient and wait for the rewards. Since they aren't disciplined, they expect quick results. They are soon to judge and give up because, according to them, things haven't turned out the way they had wanted and thus, there really isn't any point further in sticking to working hard. However, this is what the most important lesson is.

They must learn to become disciplined and have control over their emotions and feelings.

Chapter 2: What Negativity Does to Your Child?

Do you know who the biggest criticizers of your kids are? Themselves. They can and will do enough damage to themselves if the negative self-talk doesn't stop. We have to teach them how to not let their inner critic prevent them from harm. The reason negative thoughts aren't ever welcoming is that they bring along emotions like anger, frustration, and stress along with them. It may take you hours to convince them why they should look at the positive aspect of things but only a second for their inner critic to change their mind about it. The only way we can stop them is by identifying negative or harmful behaviors, which means that it has already done some of the fundamental damage. This means that we as parents, have to gear up and teach them how to look past their failures, losses, and have an optimistic mindset.

The Effects of Negativity on Our Mind and Body

During one study, researchers found that negative thinking is linked with an increased risk of developing mental health issues. This means that kids who are brought up in an environment that offers them no opportunities to grow, be positive, and achieve their dreams with determination, are likelier to suffer from mental health issues later in life (Kinderman, Schwannauer, Pontin, & Tai, 2013).

Furthermore, it can have some negative effects on the mind and body.

For instance, it can trigger hopelessness. Kids experience decreased motivation and willpower to continue with something important. They are sure of their loss from the start. This feeling of hopelessness makes an easy task seem hard and combined with a lack of motivation and drive leads to negative thoughts clouding the mind.

Negative thoughts also limit a child's thought process and problem-solving skills. They keep listening to that inner voice that takes immense pleasure in reminding them things they aren't capable of, instead of the ones they are. This limits their thinking to reason creatively and step out of the comfort zone to give something challenging a try.

Kids prone to negative thinking also believe that perfectionism is attainable. Although not entirely accomplishable, perfectionism can be a great booster to help kids aim higher. However, studies suggest that focusing too much on it can lead to increased stress about everything. Think about it this way: your child wishes to impress their new art teacher with a sketch. They want it to be perfect, so they spend more time working on it. However, every time they look at it, the more problems they find in it. So, they keep going back and forth revising and redrawing it.

A perfectionist can never be happy with what they have and tries to keep improving it. It can be quite addictive and stressful, especially for young kids.

Children with a negative outlook about life are also depressed (Schimelpfening, 2020). When left unchecked, little bouts of temporary depression can become quite damaging.

And how can we forget that the biggest and most pressing issue with negative thinking is that it isn't *positive* self-talk? Simplistic as it is, there is tons of research that positive self-talk results in good academia, a successful career, healthier well-being, and meaningful relationships (Tod, Hardy, & Oliver, 2011).

And to provide you with a rather interesting research study involving 400,000 white people and 300,000 Chinese-Americans, researchers in San Diego were astonished to look at the findings.

It all began when some researchers looked at the death records of the said amount of randomly-selected white people and Chinese Americans (Philips, Ruth & Wagner, 1993). They found that Chinese Americans died earlier than most white Americans. As it turns out, the Chinese Americans that had a combination of an ill-fated birth year (as per the Chinese astrology and medicine) and disease died five years earlier than the rest.

Researchers further dug into the causes of their deaths and concluded that the more strongly the

Chinese Americans believed in the Chinese superstitions about the ill-fated birth year, the sooner they died. The reduction in their life expectancy wasn't explainable by genetic factors, their behavior, lifestyle choices, or the skills of the doctors treating their respective diseases.

They were dying younger not due to the disease or their flawed genes but due to their strong negative beliefs. They believed that since the stars had hexed them, they were doomed to die earlier. It was nothing but their negative attitude towards life that led them to their ultimate deaths. Quite literally!

What we must notice here is the strong connection between the human brain and body. Negative emotions and stress are becoming two of the most important causes of diseases worldwide. The negativity leads to chronic stress which weakens the heart and impairs the functioning of other organs such as the lungs, kidneys, and liver. When the body is under constant stress, the body loses its balance. It becomes harder to digest and takes more time for us to heal. This makes resting difficult and the lack of rest and sleep brings more problems to the table.

Putting an End to It for Good

How can we, as parents, help our young people break this cycle of negativity and stop paying attention to that inner critic?

We, being the role models and idols they look up to, can contribute in more than one way or another to help them in this tough time. But as they say, practice what you preach, it has to start with you. If your child looks up to a parent who is always nagging about the lack of things, blaming others for their problems, and treating every new opportunity as an obstacle or challenge, they are going to pick up the same. If they see you complaining, they will complain too. If they see you being negative, they will have a negative outlook on things too. If they see you giving up your dreams because of the fear of failure or "what others will say," then they won't have the guts to try something new either. So to change them, you have to change yourself first. You will have to embrace positivity and optimism because that is how healthy habits take form. Whether you accept it or not, they are going to take after you and take up habits they see you practicing. So be the right kind of role model for your kids first and *then* preach about the power of positive thinking.

Say Positive Things to Them

As a parent, you have to help them see the positive in everything–especially when they fail at something. You have to point out the good in every circumstance whether they like it or not. The idea is to get them thinking if the outcome can be positive in some way or not. Once they start to give positive thinking a chance, it will become easier for them in the long-run. Ideally, you should radiate positivity. It allows children to see that there is another, more promising way of looking at things that don't end with frustration and sadness.

Teach Them About the Monkey Mind

Monkey Mind is an approach to view and process things. It originates from the Zen concept and suggests that since our brain works tirelessly all day long, transitions from one idea to another, listens to endless chatter both from the internal and external world, craves things, and becomes judgmental, it is very easy to get confused. So much happens in the mind that it leaves the little one confused as to what to listen to what thoughts to discard. The brain of a monkey functions in the same manner, says Dr. Arnold who introduced the concept to the world. He goes on to suggest that negative thoughts are like a monkey, climbing from one tree to another. This hinders focus on important tasks. For instance, when kids want to focus on some tasks at hand, they often get distracted. Things like procrastination, lack of focus, external distractions like noise, chatter, and people around make it harder to concentrate. All these things when amalgamated leads to negative thinking. First, procrastination delays the process, then a lack of focus makes simple tasks appear difficult, next external noises and chatter just add more pressure on the kids. Thus, they give up the task altogether.

So how to stop the monkey from climbing one tree after another and giving up everything important because it seems hard?

Dr. Arnold believes that to flip negative thinking, we must direct kids to follow these three steps.

1. Take a deep breath.
2. Tell yourself to "stop and relax" sternly.
3. And chant something positive to yourself like, "I got this" or "I can handle it."

This simple exercise can help kids break the chain of negative thoughts and replace them with something positive.

Keep a Gratitude Journal

Gratitude journals or simply listing down five things you are grateful for in life is a great way to keep the mind focused on the positives in our lives. Make it a routine to encourage the habit of keeping a gratitude journal or reminding your kids to count their blessings before going to bed so that it is the last thing they remember and wake up feeling positive and motivated.

If they aren't too keen on maintaining a gratitude journal, simply ask them to write their thoughts in a diary. The idea is to offer them a vessel to pour in their feelings. Haven't we all felt a whole lot better after discussing our problems and worries with someone? However, since most kids feel shy about taking their problems to their parents, this can work in their favor and prevent the frustration and negative thinking that builds up inside them. When they are made to feel grateful for the things they have, it changes the way they think and views things.

They start to approach things with a new sense of positivity and with elevated motivation.

Problem-Solve With Them

Keep in mind there is a big difference between problem-solving with them and for them. You have to help them come up with solutions or lead them with hints on how to do things so that they don't give up on them easily. For instance, if they are doing a puzzle, you can guide them by asking them to try putting a certain piece to check if it fits or not. The idea is to help them but make them think that they came up with it on their own. Not only does this encourage them to keep attempting and trying, but it also instills a sense of victory in them. It makes them feel confident in their abilities and with time, makes them self-reliant.

Empathize

Knowing that others understand what they are going through is another way to lessen the impact of negative thinking. Empathizing with your child allows you to show them that feeling a certain way is completely normal. It makes them feel heard and understood. When kids feel heard and cared for, they feel more supported and become more willing to give things another try in case they didn't work out the first time. For instance, saying things like, "I know you must be feeling like a complete failure to not have caught that ball in the game, but you aren't one. You will catch it the next time," can be motivating.

Switch Perspectives

"What would your favorite athlete or celebrity do if they were in this rut?"

Teaching kids to think from someone else's perspective gives their problems a new meaning and visualization. For example, if they are a fan of some rock star or footballer, ask them what they would have done in this situation. Not only does that offer some form of positive distraction, but it also helps kids try to come up with solutions on their own. After all, they wouldn't want to disappoint their favorite character. If they still seem unconvinced, ask them if their favorite rock star would have said, "I Quit" too?

Chapter 3: Am I Good Enough?

Another issue prevalent among kids is a lack of confidence. They suffer from low self-esteem and think that they aren't good enough. They rarely hone their skills and natural talents because they think there is no point to it. They often act shy and avoid social interactions, which prevents them from developing meaningful and deep connections. They feel reluctant in signing up for something new or accepting opportunities that knock on their doors. They often report feeling unloved and unwanted. You can often see them expressing negativity as they feel they are the victims of other's devilish plans. They are quick to blame others for their mistakes and don't have the strength to own up to them. When they feel frustrated, they don't know how to handle it, which means their emotional intelligence is suffering too. They are always comparing themselves with others above them and not with the ones less privileged than them. They hesitate to build new relationships due to fear of rejection and embarrassment. They also suffer from low bouts of motivation and don't take encouraging compliments well.

Noticing these signs in your little one can be heartbreaking and worrying for parents. No one wants their kids to suffer and every parent wants their child to live their lives in a more wholesome and prosperous manner. Therefore, if you are one of those parents with a kid suffering from a lack of confidence in their abilities and skills, this chapter is especially for you. Here we talk about the dangers and impacts of self-doubt on our children's lives. We see how it hurts them academically, personally, and socially. Later, we discuss the reasons that lead to low self-esteem issues in kids.

The Dangers of Self-Doubt

Our self-esteem is what reflects the way we feel about ourselves and how we approach things. Although every individual has a different level of self-esteem, it is often described as how they see their worth in the world. People who suffer from low self-esteem tend to lead a harder life as they feel incompetent at everything and thus don't approach things wholeheartedly. This means that low self-esteem affects our behavior and mood too. It is also viewable from our body language and overall demeanor towards life.

Therefore, when it comes to our children, we have to model high self-esteem from the beginning. We have to encourage and instill behaviors and habits that make them feel confident and ready. If we don't, here's how life can look for them.

Children who have self-confidence issues are unable to feel comfortable around people. This means that when we choose to not teach them how to be confident, we are depriving them of meaningful and deep relationships. Having no friends or peers to look up to can be damaging to their personality. These kids also depict avoidance behaviors, which means they are more hesitant to seek challenges or take risks than those who are taught to be confident. They have a hard time stepping out of their comfort zones and thus, fail to grow and experience many important things in life.

They can also be seen talking negatively about themselves and their abilities. They are highly critical of their appearances and talents. You can expect them to have slumped shoulders, an overall sad expression on their faces, and downcast eyes, says Joe Navarro, a former FBI counterintelligence agent during an interview with Psychology Today.

A child who suffers from poor levels of confidence also feels unskilled and incompetent when it comes to completing tasks. They are ready to give up the minute something goes against their plans and walk away. In contrast, someone with better confidence will keep on trying until they get it right and not fear failure, loss, or embarrassment.

Lastly, all these inabilities lead to a negative outlook on life. They become pessimistic and in case you didn't notice it in the earlier chapter, it can be really hard to let go of that.

What Funnels Self-Esteem Issues in Kids?

How children feel about themselves is a consequence of the things they have experienced. We all are, in fact, the product of what we experience as our experiences are what changes us–for either the good or bad. How we deal with them determines our attitude. In adolescents and teenagers, these are the following causes of poor self-esteem.

Encouragement and Support Shortfall

The foremost reason why some kids suffer from low self-esteem is that they don't feel supported or encouraged by their loved ones. These include their parents, friends, relatives, and peers. When kids don't receive adequate encouragement, they begin to internalize that they aren't good enough or wanted.

Criticism

If a child is frequently criticized for their mistakes, they start to step back from trying things and suffer from low self-confidence. Criticism from parents should come in a way that it doesn't feel humiliating or sarcastic. It should be aimed to improve and enhance their skills rather than demotivate or degrade them. The result could be a child thinking themselves incapable and incompetent.

Stressful Life Events

Have the parents recently divorced or has the family moved homes? Stressful events as such can also leave a long-lasting negative impression on a child's mind. They feel the stress is too big and find it difficult to cope.

Trauma or Abuse

When a child has been through some trauma like an accident, the loss of a parent, or from abuse (mental, emotional or physical), they begin to suffer from low self-esteem. They think that nothing good will ever happen to them and feel like they have been truly cursed. So they basically just give up on life and all that it has to offer, thinking, "what's the point, anyways."

Bullying

Being bullied, either at school, among friends or at home can also hurt a child's self-esteem. They shouldn't be made to feel like they aren't worthy of the good things or are just a nuisance in the lives of others. This can trigger isolation and social distancing, which leads to loneliness and depression as they grow older.

Negative Comparisons

Do you often compare your kids with your friends' kids or with their friends? You want them to be like them, which sounds like a good idea to you, but it isn't. Kids who feel like they have to live up to someone else to be considered intelligent or smart also suffer from low self-esteem. Basically, when we tell them to be like someone else, we are really telling them to give up on who they are and change. This too can foster negativity in them and they may forever feel inept.

Unrealistic Expectations

Setting unachievable goals in life is another way to inflict low self-esteem in kids. The pressure to be a certain someone can come from parents, peers, teachers, or friends. Imposing unrealistic expectations means that they will constantly struggle to meet them and probably fail. The failure ensures that they were indeed right about their poor skills and abilities.

Chapter 4: I Am Confident and Self-Reliant

Confidence comes from positive outcomes. Positive outcomes fuel confidence as they serve as motivators. When we put our heart and soul into something, say like a new recipe, and it turns out amazing and bags us compliments from our spouse and kids, don't we feel confident? Doesn't that give us the motivation to try something new the next day?

It helps kids improve in the same manner too. When something they did reaps positive outcomes, they feel more confident and self-reliant. When they feel confident and assured, they feel empowered to invest their time and resources in other things too. Confidence is what makes kids persistent. Without, we give up soon or simply don't start at all. So in a way, we can say that it is what saves kids from despair and hopelessness.

The Barriers to Self-Confidence in Kids

However, there are some barriers when encouraging kids to be self-confident. Before we head straight into teaching you strategies to help empower your kids to become confident adults, it is only fair to know of and eliminate the factors that pose hurdles in our efforts.

Self-Defeating Assumptions

Some kids just think that they can't, so they don't try. Sometimes, they become so rattled by a little inconvenience that they call quits to the next one without even a single attempt. They decide to let go of something, assuming they won't be able to have it. For instance, a child may decide to learn to play baseball. However, every time they try to play catch with their older sibling, they miss all catches. So, they decide to not join the school team–assuming they will be bad at it. These are what we call, self-defeating assumptions. It's good to be realistic but that doesn't mean you start to act like a loser before even trying. Kids who believe in such self-defeating assumptions can be hard to train.

Setting Unrealistic Goals

On the contrary, some kids act like big shows and take up more than they could handle. It's ambitious to tackle BHAGs (big hairy audacious goals) but only if you are prepared for it. Enormous goals often undermine confidence. This can stem from demotivation and depression. Confidence is something that mostly comes from small wins at first.

Celebrating Too Soon

Do you have a child who celebrates their weight loss by eating an entire cake? What kind of celebration is it? Kids who claim to be victors before reaching their end goals can trigger a lack of confidence when they fail at the next stage. For instance, your kid scores high grades in math during a class test. So, they confidently announce it to the whole class that they will be one getting the highest grade in math in the finals. Seems the right kind of anticipation, right? But before the finals, they have to score high in the next test too, which they don't. And then there goes their confidence out of the door.

Blaming Others

Kids who don't own up to their mistakes and instead blame others for their mishaps are also hard to train. They, themselves are the barrier to building confidence as they aren't willing to listen and make amends to their behavior and thoughts. Even when wronged by someone, we still have the choice to either cry about it or make a difference for ourselves. Sadly, kids who choose the first often report having poor confidence and show resistance when schooled about it.

Not Anticipating Setbacks

A child who doesn't anticipate setbacks and moves forward with blind optimism may stumble and fall hard on their head. Optimism is a good thing but when it clouds the mind of a child, they forget about the dangers and challenges along the way. Therefore, when something unexpected happens, they lose their confidence and edge. This is the hardest to treat as they have had a taste of positivity before and now have turned bitter and hopeless.

Being Overconfident

There is a fine line between being confident and arrogant and kids who don't understand that, often end up crossing it. Arrogance can lead to neglecting the basics, turning a deaf ear to the critics, and being blinded by the forces of change.

Learning to Shut the Inner Voice

All kids need positive affirmations to defeat the inner critic. As parents, we can help them find that positivity and turn their negative perceptions into something positive and progressive. First off, we must use language that reeks of positivity, even when they feel down. This kind of outlook about everything is what they are going to pick up too and use to uplift their confidence. Other than that:

You must, at all times, love them. This seems rather debatable as every parent thinks they love their child unconditionally. True, but sometimes we forget to show it to them. Love demands actions and actions drive behavior. Dole out plenty of love their way to encourage them and make them realize that they always have a strong support system behind them. This also means putting an end to baseless comparisons and extremely high expectations that they will fail to meet. Every child, including yours, needs to feel accepted and looked after. When we yell, shout, or ignore them, we are unconsciously undermining their level of confidence. Ever had your child come up to you to show you how well they have colored the drawing? They are attention-seekers naturally and when they don't get that, "Wow, this looks amazing. Let's hang it on the fridge for daddy to see," they lose their confidence.

This takes us to the second important practice and that is, praising them when it's due. Holding back praise is another reason why some kids suffer from a lack of confidence in their lives. Positive feedback, even for adults, is an essential thing to have. So why deprive our kids of it? Praise them even if they have repeated the same practice for the hundredth time. Because what you don't know is that when they feel encouraged and praised, they try to do it better than the last time. Praises can also result in repeated actions, which is the perfect way to develop new habits such as persistence, resilience, and improved confidence.

Speaking of resilience, your child must also be taught that success isn't always a guarantee. This means there is a chance of setbacks and unexpected failures and pain. But they must know how to overcome and cope with such hardships without losing their confidence. Teaching resilience also means we promote the act of moving forward and not dwell on the failures for too long. More on this in Chapter 7, so stay tuned!

Next, you must, at all times and by all means, foster a growth mindset. Unlike a fixed mindset that suggests that humans are born with all the talents and skills they will ever possess, a growth mindset strongly believes in the possibility of learning new skills and cultivating talents over time. This is the kind of mindset you need your child to have.

Another way to build confidence is to help them in pursuing their passions. It is a no-secret secret that everyone acts more driven and passionate when it comes to doing something they love or are a fan of. Say, your child loves to draw. If you encourage them to follow their passion, take up additional advanced courses to improve their skills, they will feel more confident.

And finally, while helping them build confidence, don't forget to set goals that are achievable and tell them what is expected of them. Set uncomplicated rules that they can follow easily and don't be too hard on them when they fail to follow them. The goal shouldn't be to enforce rules and be strict, but to help them work around any setbacks and offer more clarity. When they know what is expected of them and how to get there, they will feel more confident.

Chapter 5: Taming the Monster Under the Bed

Did you know, one in every eight kids is affected by some type of anxiety? Untreated anxiety can develop into disorders, is hard to treat, and often results in poor school performance, increased absences, and missing out of important social experiences. Some research studies also suggest that it can drive kids and teenagers towards substance abuse (Lander, Howsare, & Byrne, 2013).

Anxiety is sometimes a fairly normal reaction to a given situation. Despite being seen as something bad, it needs to be comprehended as something preventive if it happens. All kids, big or small, experience anxiety at some point in their lives. It can be on graduation day, during an exam, or just when asked to make an introduction to the class. It has many phases that come and go. Think of a phase as something temporary. This means that it isn't harmful. However, kids who experience anxiety also report the development of other emotions like fear, shyness, or nervousness—emotions that can hinder their overall quality of life.

Some Common Signs of Anxiety

So, what does anxiety look like and how can parents know if their kids are being anxious or just excited?

There are some common signs to look for. For instance, a kid who suffers from bouts of anxiety may often cling onto someone (in the case that they are little), act scared or upset, cry, miss school, and be silent. They may also show a resistance when told to do something or do it wrong because their mind isn't where it should be. It is off somewhere wandering about the stress they are subconsciously experiencing. Some easy to notice symptoms include sweating, a worried look on their face, or nervousness that leads to shivering, shaking, or a racing heart.

When it starts to affect the body, that is when you really need to start worrying because anxiety can trigger a panic attack, which can make it harder for them to breathe. They may also complain of stomach aches or a dry mouth.

These symptoms that we associate with an anxious mind trigger the flight or fight response in the body. This is a normal response to an external threat or danger and humans have been experiencing it for ages. Anxiety releases chemicals in the brain that affect our nervous and digestive systems–preparing them to suit up for a fight. However, when anxiety attacks, this fight or flight response becomes overactive. So even when there is no danger present, the body tricks the mind into thinking there is and that is when all hell breaks loose.

Can Anxiety Be a Good Thing?

All that we have told you up to now about anxiety might have caused you to believe that it is a very bad thing. It is, most of the time. But there are times when this very emotion is the one that leads to greatness. Before we prepare parents to treat the symptoms of anxiety in their kids, how about we take a look at the claim we just made above.

Could anxiety be good?

Scientists believe that some extent of it is (Parker & Ragsdale, 2015). Referred to as eustress, good stress can serve as a motivating factor. There are some silver linings to it too and before wasting any more time, let's learn what they could be.

Anxiety can signal a warning. For instance, it can tell a child playing baseball, when to hit the ball or how to read the mind of the pitcher to anticipate the kind of swing they need to take. It brings awareness to the present and somehow slows down our minds to take in more information. Think of it as a slow-motion shot in a movie. Recurring worry and anxiety are signs that things need to change in your life and that your current state doesn't make you happy. When this happens, the child starts to explore ways and strategies to cope with it.

It can also serve as motivation as stated above. For instance, a child preparing for an exam the night before it is happening. Some level of anxiety about their exam will keep them focused on the revisions and enhance cognitive performance.

Anxiety also prepares us to battle a threat. Our bodies are wired to protect ourselves from danger and survive against all odds. When kids are faced with a challenge or tough situation and the anxiety creeps in, it can help them become more agile, process more information and radiate more energy. Notice how right after an accident, some bystanders can lift a full-size car and save the victim's life? That is anxiety doing its thing

What Can I Do to Help My Child?

Sometimes, when kids suffer from chronic anxiety that keeps them stuck under the covers out of fear, it can be hard for parents to cope. No one wants to see their kids suffer, especially from something they seemingly can't do anything about. In an effort to help them cope, they end up exacerbating it further. This is most common when parents try to take control and protect them from anticipated anxiety. But it isn't always the right thing to do. The goal should be to teach them how to cope with it on their own so that the next time they face it, they know what to do about it.

To help you get started, here are a few things you can do to calm them down.

Reassure Them

Worry is inevitable. If you know your child is worrying, no point in telling them not to worry. It seems like the right thing to do but what you have to do instead is, reassure them. Try to rationalize the worry using the FEEL method. The benefit of the feel method is that when kids are feeling stressed, their brain releases a dump of chemicals that makes them turn deaf to all the advice being given. It's not like they don't want to hear or listen to you, it's just that their brain doesn't allow them to. The prefrontal cortex, regulating logic and rationale goes numb and thus, they are unable to think clearly. This is where the FEEL method comes in. It stands for:

F: Freeze: The first thing you need to do is to tell them to pause and take deep breaths.

E: Empathize: Tell them that you understand what they are going through without offering any advice or suggestion. Just let them know that you get it.

E: Evaluate: This includes the task of problem-solving with them to find solutions to the problems. This comes after they are done being anxious and are all calmed down.

L: Let Go: This last one is for you, parents. In case you aren't successful in helping your child cope, don't let the guilt consume you. Let go of the notion that you are a bad parent.

Build a Relaxation Kit With Them

The best way to de-stress is to distract the young one with something else. For you, it might mean going for a walk or taking a bubble bath. For your kids, it can mean doing something they like doing. For example, if they love to color, you can create a kit including some drawing books and color boxes. If they are a fan of playing with action figures, you can have a bag full of them hanging behind their room's door.

These are meant to be relaxation kits, involving things they enjoy doing or are interested in. This will divert their mind and reduce the amount of anxiety they feel.

Talk It Out

If they are old enough to understand the emotion they are going through, there is nothing better than to have a talk with them about it like adults. They should know what is happening to their body and why. When kids don't understand that what they are going through is anxiety, it can be frightening. On the other hand, when they know what they have to deal with, they feel much more prepared and confident. Sit them down and help them recognize the feelings and triggers that induce anxiety. Reassure them that this will pass.

DIY a Worry Box

It doesn't have to be a box; it can also be a jar. The idea is to give them an activity that helps them recognize, analyze, and cope with what they are feeling. The trick is to write down the cause of the worry on a piece of paper and put it in the worry box. Tell them to take out the paper a week later and see if the worry is still there or worth causing anxiety. If it isn't, they can simply tear up the paper and feel freed from it.

Respect Their Feelings

If a child seems stressed about some upcoming event, respect their feelings but don't empower them. They should learn to deal with the event and be more prepared to face it. Validation is one thing and agreeing with them is another. So simply acknowledge but don't offer solutions. Let them come up with some on their own.

Chapter 6: Call Upon the Stage—Willpower

As kids grow, they face new challenges every day. In this fast-paced and competitive world, they have to rise above others to find their place in the world. When they feel confident enough to head for achievement, they need persistence and perseverance. These two require a ton of self-discipline and willpower.

Willpower or self-discipline refers to the ability to delay or avoid unhealthy excess of things. We have been told repeatedly throughout our lives that excess of anything is bad. One of the biggest advantages of self-discipline in the life of a child is that it allows them to willingly give up on the easy way of doing things and focus on doing them right. This eliminates shortcuts and instant gratification, which many opt for. However, self-disciplined kids know that the harder they work, the greater will be the reward. So they stay put, focus on the task at hand and don't give in to distractions—positive or negative.

We can understand self-discipline and willpower in several ways. The definitions of both are synonymously used to determine:

- The ability to not give up
- Perseverance
- Self-control

- Staying focused on the goals despite setbacks and failures

What Disciplining a Child Means

Discipline means teaching a child about guidelines, expectations, and principles. Children need to be regularly taught how to differentiate between what is good and bad for them. There are many ways to teach discipline. Some ways focus on increasing positive behaviors or decreasing undesirable ones. Others include the concept of rewards and punishments. Whichever method is used, the goal remains the same. It is to foster sound judgment in children so that they feel more confident to navigate their paths in life. Disciplining a child means that they learn to control their desires, negative emotions and feelings and learn to be responsible for their actions. It also means that they know that their actions will have consequences, so they need to be extra cautious about the choices they make. It also aims to teach them to own up to their mistakes but not hold onto them for the rest of their lives or quit because of them.

But how can it help beat negative behavior? How can we be sure that teaching them about having strong willpower will save them from any negative thoughts or at least, allow them to escape from them?

Beating Negativity With Self-Control

To beat negativity, your child just needs one thing–the right mindset or attitude. Attitude refers to the way we dedicated ourselves to how we think. If we think negatively, we will have a negative outlook on everything. If we think positively, we will notice the beauty in everything, even the things that are flawed. It's like your child's bicycle with pedals and brakes. If they want to stop, they can stop. If they want to keep going, they can keep going. It all comes down to their choice and self-control.

Below are some ideal tips and practices to start with your kid/kids so that they maintain a positive outlook or to put it more accurately–nip negativity before it starts to branch out and corrupt their little minds.

Teach them to be open and accept their mistakes. They need to come clean about when they make an oopsie and own it. Blaming others won't get them far, it will only make them feel like a victim. The first step they will take is to take responsibility for their actions and then for their emotions.

Secondly, let them know that they always have a choice. They can either call it quits or keep moving ahead. It is up to them. When discussing this, focus heavily on the positive aspects of moving forward and the drawbacks of giving up.

Teach them to look at mistakes and failures as lessons and not as roadblocks. If you want to beat negativity with strong willpower, then they must know that it is their thoughts that direct their actions. If they view their failures as a means of learning, they will know what mistakes to avoid making in the future. If they view them as crappy and stupid, they will choose to quit.

Give them examples of people they can look up to. Give them resources to learn about aspiring people. When they learn about the hardships these people had to go through and how, despite those difficulties, they made a name for themselves, it will motivate them to do the same.

Tell them to have an empathetic approach. The more giving and caring they are, the more they will be rewarded. Have you ever noticed how good things keep happening to good people? It is their thinking and humble approach towards others that win them a place in the world and in the hearts of others.

Help them come up with solutions, distractions, and ways to shift their gaze to the bright side of things. If they focus too much on what they don't have instead of what they do, they will always remain crybabies and worry too much. Teach them to see the glass as half-full and not half-empty.

And finally, let them know that complaining won't get them anywhere. If they aren't happy with something, they better create change. It is the only way to come out of a negative solution as a victor.

Chapter 7: Resilience to the Rescue

Imagine a world free from peer pressure, bullying, diseases, poverty, or death. Imagine if we had the power to save our kids from all such nuisances and cruel realities of life. Wouldn't that make it a much happier world to live in?

Since we unfortunately can't, we have to ensure that if the time comes, they are ready to take care of themselves, their feelings, and emotions. As parents, we want to protect them from everything that is bad, but for how long? How can we do that when they fly away from the nest and start their own families, careers, and separate lives? Our worries would still be the same. One of the biggest things anyone fears is change. And kids, well, they don't do well with it either. But change is inevitable. This means we have to work harder to prepare them for the unknown and life's uncertainties. We have to prepare them to not only face hardships and challenges and come out as victors but also to accept their failures and move on.

A resilient child is someone who knows how to bounce back from loss, grief, or failure. For them, it isn't just about surviving but rather viewing the negative outcomes and finding something positive in them. It is the uniqueness of resilient kids that unlike others, they are able to thrive and grow–no matter how big the setbacks.

Building resilience in kids is important for a number of reasons. For starters, it allows them to develop habits and coping mechanisms that will come in handy whenever they are faced with a challenging task or unexpected loss. It will prevent them from becoming overwhelmed by their emotions and let them determine the next course of action. Any step not taken with the right mind can have bitter consequences. Therefore, resilience helps kids find that balance in between their emotions and actions and come out of stressful times tactfully.

Secondly, resilience also allows kids to make healthy and calculated risks. They can do so because failure no longer seems like a threat. They don't fear the unexpected and are accepting of their mistakes when they make them. They also feel more confident to move beyond their comfort zones and explore daring options. In general, they are brave, curious and trust their instincts. All of these qualities aid them in achieving their goals and following their passions.

Resilient kids also face fewer mental health issues later in life. Although there is only some emerging evidence to imply a link, we still believe it possible. First, kids with mental health issues, such as chronic anxiety or depression have a negative outlook on life. They hold onto their past, mistakes, and failures. A lack of resilience renders them helpless to overcome them. So we can sense a pattern there.

How Resilience Beats Anxiety and Negativity

But the real question is this: can it beat anxiety and negativity? If you are looking for a one-word answer, then yes. Strong resilience and toughness can help get rid of negative thoughts. There are a few ideas worth sharing to help parents teach their children. These are aimed to help their children beat the crippling effects of anxiety and negativity on their mind and body.

Offer Them a Healthy Environment

As their parent, your foremost duty is to give them a healthy environment to survive in. They should engage in activities that help them stay calm and relaxed. They should be able to express themselves and be heard. They should be able to spend quality time with their parents and siblings fostering care, compassion, and affection. They should always feel supported and looked after.

Focus on Their Well-Being

Any child, who feels cared for and loved will be optimistic. Being loved by others offers us a sense of comfort. Your goal here should be to build a strong emotional connection with them. This requires that you help them problem-solve, listen to their worries and concerns, and show empathy. When children feel loved, they feel empowered to take chances. They know that they have a strong support system backing them and thus, they feel more confident to approach new things. It also builds their coping skills with negative emotions like anger, frustration, angst, or sadness.

Offer Opportunities to Take Healthy Risks

Parents should also offer their children a chance to step out of their comfort zones and indulge in something that challenges them. In a world when we have made playgrounds safe by installing bouncy floors, it is very hard to find ways to encourage them to take healthy risks. Healthy risk is something that doesn't involve too much danger but still allows the child with an opportunity to grow and learn. For instance, encouraging them to ride their bike without training wheels could be a start. This builds resilience in them over time, especially when they succeed.

Reframe Bad Experiences

Help kids see bad experiences in a more positive light. Ask them what they learned from those events and what changes they are planning to make to counter any mistakes the next time. Healthy discussions as such, open room for a new and improved perspective. Motivate them to look for the silver lining in all things–even failures and heartbreaks. If your teenage son just had a tough breakup, ask him to look at the reasons why it wasn't perfect in the first place and remind him not to repeat the errors the next time. Not only will it help with healing, but it will also build resilience.

Teach Them the Art of Letting Go

Lastly, to beat negativity, children have to learn to let go of the things in the past and focus on their present and future. The best way to outdo negativity is to give today a chance to be better. Teach them to acknowledge, accept, and let go of what happened in the past and move on. When they start to focus on their today and tomorrow, they will experience reduced stress and more anticipation for a happy future.

Chapter 8: Is My Child Emotionally Ready?

It is every parent's ultimate goal to raise an emotionally intelligent child. Emotional-intelligence, unlike general IQ, doesn't get enough limelight. However, it is starting to. This final chapter aims to give parents an overall idea about what emotional intelligence is, why their kids need it and how it can help break the cycle of negativity.

You must have noticed that nearly all the chapters before this have dealt with issues of either negative attitudes or anxiety. But we are yet to discuss what happens when negativity wins, when anxiety and stress get the best of our kids, and when the day seems less happy as we see our kids defeated by the hand of their inner critic. Who is responsible for what comes next? Why doesn't no one talk about the damage that happens afterward?

The foremost reason to raise emotionally-intelligent kids is so that they can manage the many emotions they experience and learn to regulate them on their own. Being emotionally intelligent allows kids to prevent a meltdown or temper tantrum before it happens and cope with their failures, loss, or grief in a more dignified and productive manner.

Understanding Emotional Intelligence

Emotional intelligence is an individual's ability to express, control, handle, and be conscious of the emotions they feel. It entails the art of being considerate towards ourselves and others and speak our minds better. On the whole, these are the things that an emotionally-intelligent child will portray. They can:

- Recognize and analyze the emotions of others and themselves.
- Possess emotional consciousness.
- Label their emotions and know how to express them.
- Understand how feelings and emotions affect mood, physical health, voice, body language, and state of mind.
- Build emotional vocabulary to better name the emotion they are experiencing.
- Bridge the gap between actions and emotions and how the latter can affect the former.
- Show sympathy towards others and be empathetic towards them.

Statistics reveal that nearly 10% of kids across the globe suffer from depression. This is alarming as we still don't have a cure for chronic depression. The kids who are depressed fail to deal with the emotions they feel, and thus, have an overall negative thought process. When one is depressed, the creative and rational parts of the brain become suppressed. This renders us hopeless when it comes to coping with what we feel and helpless in looking for a solution to counter it. Therefore, it is becoming highly crucial in today's age that we teach our children how to develop emotional intelligence and use it as a tool to combat negativity.

How a Mentally-Tough Mind Makes Combating Negativity Easier

Kids experience a wide range of emotions. These include both the positive and the negative. Usually, positive emotions are rewarded with praise, appreciation, and satisfaction. It is the other set of emotions that pose the real threat. Kids experience negative emotions too. Perhaps, someone from their class, other than them, got selected as the teacher's helper. Perhaps, someone well-deserving got kicked off the football team. Perhaps, they found out that their best friend wasn't a friend at all. It is okay to feel a range of negative emotions in these instances. There are endless scenarios we can list that breed negative emotions.

So how do we, as their parents, help them cope with those emotions better? How, using emotional intelligence, we can teach them to work through them without taking any drastic actions?

Is It Really Worth It?

Ask them if the problems they are facing now will be worth crying over in the future? Will an insignificant failure, like failing a class test, matter when they are older? Kids need to know to regulate their emotions from an early age. They must be made to understand which things are worth the effort and which aren't. If they experience a setback, ask them if it somehow hinders their long-term goals or not. Ask them, is it worth crying their out eyes over it? Ask them if it is worth the fight or would you be better off using your energy on something worthy? Knowing how the emotions they feel today determine their actions and possible outcomes in the future can help them make better choices.

Label the Feelings

When kids know what they are feeling, they can better feel the power they have over them. They need to be able to distinguish between anger and frustration, sadness and grief, worry and anxiety. When they know what they are dealing with, they cope with it better.

What Is the Other Person Thinking?

If the negative emotion involves someone other than your child, tell them to try wearing the other person's shoes for a moment and look at the situation from their perspective. For instance, if your child felt hurt because their friend didn't let them ride their new bike, ask them would they have done the same?

Would they have allowed someone else to ride it, considering how choosy they are?

Viewing things from someone else's perspectives breeds a sense of empathy–an integral part of emotional intelligence. Your child will get an insider's look at how it feels like to be on the other end of the spectrum for once and build empathy and concern. They will also be less judgmental about things and try to view them from various mindsets too.

Prevents Immature Reactions

When kids know what they are feeling and why they are feeling it, it prevents them from reacting immediately or too hastily. When they are taught that reacting to a negative emotion never results in a positive outcome, they avoid reacting to them with an outburst. Instead, they look for means to cope with them and healthily distance themselves from them.

Conclusion

Throughout the book, we have labeled negative thoughts as bad or unwanted. However, did you know that if we never experienced them, we wouldn't have been able to make the distinction between which are good and which are bad for us? Keeping that in mind, it doesn't mean that we let our children experience negativity all the time. We need to teach them to manage it and keep it at bay. If we don't, it will wash away all their happy memories and opportunities of growth.

In this book, not only did we look at how to beat negative thoughts, but we also briefly discussed negativity's many friends that tag along with it. These include anxiety, stress, lack of self-confidence, poor resilience, and low self-esteem. All these emotions and disorders are the offspring of negative thinking. Therefore, to get rid of a negative mind and approach, we needed to tackle these first. And we did, hopefully!

We listed such means and strategies that will make parenting seem slightly less taxing and help parents raise optimistic and self-reliant kids. We also provided strategies and ways to nurture self-confidence in children so that they can prepare themselves for the world. There is not a doubt in our minds that by adopting these practices, our kids will learn to become resilient in the face of adversity and uncertainty and cope with negative emotions intelligently and empathetically.

Now that we feel more empowered, it is time we let the world know that we are ready to send our little soldiers out the door, sit back, and watch them succeed.

Thank you for giving this book a read. I hope you loved reading it as much as I enjoyed writing it. It would make me the happiest person on earth if you would take a moment to leave an honest review. All you have to do is visit the site where you purchased this book: It's that simple! The review doesn't have to be a full-fledged paragraph; a few words will do. Your few words will help others decide if this is what they should be reading as well. Thank you in advance, and best of luck with your parenting adventures. Every moment is a joyous one with a child.

References

10 Tips for Parenting Anxious Children. (2016, February 29). Retrieved from https://www.webmd.com/parenting/features/10-tips-parenting-anxious-children

Deutschendorf, H. (2019, November 12). 5 Ways Emotional Intelligence Helps Us Manage Negative Emotions. Retrieved from https://thriveglobal.com/stories/5-ways-emotional-intelligence-helps-us-manage-negative-emotions/

Jain, R. (2017, September 7). 9 Things Every Parent with an Anxious Child Should Try. Retrieved from https://www.huffpost.com/entry/9-things-every-parent-with-an-anxious-child-should-try_b_5651006

Kanter, R. M. (2019, November 6). Overcome the Eight Barriers to Confidence. Retrieved from https://hbr.org/2014/01/overcome-the-eight-barriers-to-confidence

Kinderman, P., Schwannauer, M., Pontin, E., & Tai, S. (2013). Psychological Processes Mediate the Impact of Familial Risk, Social Circumstances and Life Events on Mental Health. PLoS ONE.

Lander, L., Howsare, J., & Byrne, M. (2013). The Impact of Substance Use Disorders on

Families and Children: From Theory to Practice. Social work in public health, 194–205.

O'Shea, E. (2020, March 20). 6 Tips to Help your Negative Child. Retrieved from https://www.parent4success.com/2014/03/19/6-tips-to-help-your-negative-child/

Parker, K. N., & Ragsdale, J. M. (2015). Effects of Distress and Eustress on Changes in Fatigue from Waking to Working. Applied Psychology: Health and Well-Being , 293-315.

Schimelpfening, N. (2020, March 21). Symptoms of Clinical Depression. Retrieved from Verywell Mind: https://www.verywellmind.com/top-depression-symptoms-1066910

Star, K. (2019, September 29). Are There Potential Benefits to Having Anxiety? Retrieved from https://www.verywellmind.com/benefits-of-anxiety-2584134#citation-1

Tod, D., Hardy, J., & Oliver, E. J. (2011). Effects of Self-Talk: A Systematic Review. Journal of Sport and Exercise Psychology, 666-87.

Made in the USA
Middletown, DE
09 June 2022

66875225R00044